Andrey Artyushin

Greater Than a Tourist Book Ser

C000058750

I think the series is wonderful and beneficial for tourists to get information before visiting the city.

-Seckin Zumbul, Izmir Turkey

I am a world traveler who has read many trip guides but this one really made a difference for me. I would call it a heartfelt creation of a local guide expert instead of just a guide.

-Susy, Isla Holbox, Mexico

New to the area like me, this is a must have!

-Joe, Bloomington, USA

This is a good series that gets down to it when looking for things to do at your destination without having to read a novel for just a few ideas.

-Rachel, Monterey, USA

Good information to have to plan my trip to this destination.

-Pennie Farrell, Mexico

Aptly titled, you won't just be a tourist after reading this book. You'll be greater than a tourist!

-Alan Warner, Grand Rapids, USA

Thank you for a fantastic book.

-Don, Philadelphia, USA

Great ideas for a port day.

-Mary Martin USA

Even though I only have three days to spend in San Miguel in an upcoming visit, I will use the author's suggestions to guide some of my time there. An easy read - with chapters named to guide me in directions I want to go.

-Robert Catapano, USA

Great insights from a local perspective! Useful information and a very good value!

-Sarah, USA

This series provides an in-depth experience through the eyes of a local. Reading these series will help you to travel the city in with confidence and it'll make your journey a unique one.

-Andrew Teoh, Ipoh, Malaysia

Tourists can get an amazing "insider scoop" about a lot of places from all over the world. While reading, you can feel how much love the writer put in it.

-Vanja Živković, Sremski Karlovci, Serbia

Andrey Artyushin

GREATER THAN A TOURIST – MOSCOW RUSSIA

50 Travel Tips from a Local

Andrey Artyushin

Cover designed by Lisa Rusczyk Ed. D.

Greater Than a Tourist
Visit our website at www.GreaterThanaTourist.com

Lock Haven, PA

ISBN: 9781973256335

Andrey Artyushin

>TOURIST

50 TRAVEL TIPS FROM A LOCAL

Andrey Artyushin

BOOK DESCRIPTION

Are you excited about planning your next trip?
Do you want to try something new?
Would you like some guidance from a local?

If you answered yes to any of these questions, then this Greater Than a Tourist book is for you.

Greater Than a Tourist – Moscow by Andrey Artyushin offers the inside scoop on the capital of Russia. Most travel books tell you how to travel like a tourist. Although there is nothing wrong with that, as part of the Greater Than a Tourist series, this book will give you travel tips from someone who has lived at your next travel destination.

In these pages you'll discover advice that will help you throughout your stay. This book will not tell you exact addresses or store hours but instead will give you excitement and knowledge from a local that you may not find in other smaller print travel books.

Travel like a local. Slow down, stay in one place, and get to know the people and the culture. By the time you finish this book, you will be eager and prepared to travel to your next destination.

>TOURIST

Andrey Artyushin

TABLE OF CONTENTS

TOP REASONS TO BOOK THIS TRIP

> TOURIST

GREATER THAN A TOURIST

> TOURIST

GREATER THAN A TOURIST

NOTEs

Andrey Artyushin

DEDICATION

This book is dedicated to Oleg, who supported me while I was writing it. And Haennim, who tried to, I think.

>TOURIST

Andrey Artyushin

ABOUT THE AUTHOR

Andrey Artyushin was born and poorly raised in Moscow, and then left it to see what's outside. He has been selling cars, managing a charity, playing in a band, owning an online store, working in a bank, giving lectures, and selling pastry. He is also a lieutenant of Russian Rocket Forces. Now he works as a copywriter wherever they want him to, but checks on home regularly to see what's new in Mother Russia.

One of Andrey's greatest pleasures is seeing the shocked faces of foreigners every time they learn firsthand that "yes, Russia is different". Another one is good vodka.

Andrey doesn't consider himself an expert on anything. But he knows places. Fun places, interesting places, tasty places. And he doesn't mind sharing.

>TOURIST

Andrey Artyushin

HOW TO USE THIS BOOK

The Greater Than a Tourist book series was written by someone who has lived in an area for over three months. The goal of this book is to help travelers either dream or experience different locations by providing opinions from a local. The author has made suggestions based on their own experiences. Please do your own research before traveling to the area in case the suggested places are unavailable.

>TOURIST

Andrey Artyushin

FROM THE PUBLISHER

Traveling can be one of the most important parts of a person's life. The anticipation and memories that you have are some of the best. As a publisher of the Greater Than a Tourist book series, as well as the popular 50 Things to Know book series, we strive to help you learn about new places, spark your imagination, and inspire you. Wherever you are and whatever you do I wish you safe, fun, and inspiring travel.

Lisa Rusczyk Ed. D.
CZYK Publishing

>TOURIST

Andrey Artyushin

OUR STORY

Traveling is a passion of the "Greater than a Tourist" series creator. Lisa studied abroad in college, and for their honeymoon Lisa and her husband toured Europe. During her travels to Malta, an older man tried to give her some advice based on his own experience living on the island since he was a young boy. She was not sure if she should talk to the stranger but was interested in his advice. When traveling to some places she was wary to talk to locals because she was afraid that they weren't being genuine. Through her travels, Lisa learned how much locals had to share with tourists. Lisa created the "Greater Than a Tourist" book series to help connect people with locals. A topic that locals are very passionate about sharing.

>TOURIST

Andrey Artyushin

WELCOME TO
> TOURIST

>TOURIST

INTRODUCTION

*In Moscow you sit in a huge room at a restaurant; you know no one
and no one knows you, and at the same time you don't feel a stranger.*
-Anton Chekhov

Moscow is crazy. Russia is crazy. Life is crazy.

I really hope this book will help to bring some order into your trip
to this ADHD city.

The book starts with some general tips, then moves on to sights and
landmarks, and then gives you places to eat and fun stuff to do for
desserts. These are not nearly all the places you can visit, and not even
all the typical tourist spots. But these are the places that are fun,
interesting, unusual, and worth getting the Russian visa for.

I don't expect you to learn to read Russian. I included both the way
names of the locations are pronounced in Russian and the way they are
spelled with Cyrillic letters so that you can just point at the word in
your book in the likely case that your Russian pronunciation isn't too
understandable.

Have fun and be bold, and you'll come back with a lot of wild
stories to tell.

>TOURIST

Andrey Artyushin

1. FORGET EVERYTHING YOU KNOW ABOUT MOSCOW

If you have an image of a frozen grey city full of grumpy white people in your head, you probably watch Hollywood movies too much. Let me give you some updates.

Being the enormous country it is, Russian Federation has people of more than 190 nationalities living in it. And you can find all of them and more among the 20 million of people roaming the streets of Moscow every day.

You can find all kinds of architectural styles here too. A mosque next to an orthodox church next to a modern business center next to a 19th-century mansion – just another Moscow side street. It's a city of contrasts and chaos, and you can travel through time and continents just by crossing into another district.

It's easy to get lost here, but easy to find a friendly stranger to help you out as well. It's a common stereotype that Russians don't smile. We actually do, a lot - but only when we mean it. Just be nice, and we'll be the most hospitable people you've ever met.

Welcome to Moscow! Enjoy your time in this perfect spot for an adventure.

2. WHICH SEASON TO CHOOSE?

Yes, we really do have summers in Moscow. It starts getting warm around mid-April and stays relatively comfy outside until mid – September when it's a good year. But the temperature varies greatly throughout the year, so you can both drown in sweat at +40°C and become a human icicle at -25°C.

Summer Moscow will pleasantly surprise you. It's bright, it's green, it's beautiful. People dance in the parks, people drink in the parks, what's not to enjoy?
Seriously, if you want to see more of Moscow, come in summer or late spring. You will be able to actually walk or even **sit** outside, instead of running from one warm place to another. And the city bike rental system only works when it's warm, too.

However, winter in Moscow also has its plus sides. The city is decorated for the New Year celebrations in December, and there are tons of street markets to get a cup of mulled wine at. Ice skating rinks also pop up in parks all around Moscow. So, if you aren't scared of Russian winters, get your warm clothes out and enjoy the romance of the snow.

3. BE PREPARED

If you don't speak Russian and don't know anyone who does, it might be a bit difficult for you. Most signs and shop names are written in Russian. That means **with Cyrillic letters.** Learning how to read those in advance might help you a great deal, but you don't have to.

Just try making sure you know the exact locations or at least the names of places you want to go to. The city center has signs pointing to the main tourist attractions in English, so that might help if you get lost. But if you find yourself lost somewhere on the outskirts, you might be in trouble. You can always find the nearest subway station and check the map there – names of the stations are dubbed in English too.

If you have to ask for directions, younger people are more likely to speak English. But having an offline map can definitely help. You can download one in advance for the areas you need with the Google Maps app.

4. HOW TO PAY FOR STUFF

The currency is called the ruble, and its foreign exchange rate has had a lot of fun adventures in the recent years. Not really that fun for Russians, unfortunately. For now, the rate is around 70 rubles per 1 euro and around 60 rubles per 1 dollar. Try not to exchange your money at airports or train stations, though; the rates there are far from fair.

You will have to get some cash because you won't be able to pay with your credit cards in many places. As most Russians use the same bank, they often transfer the money online on the spot to pay for things. But your safest bet is definitely having some rubles in your pocket.

Counting your change is a good idea for sure. Russians usually think that foreign tourists don't care about money at all, so some local vendors think that keeping some of your change is a fair way of helping you do some charity.

5. GETTING FROM THE AIRPORT

In case you didn't know, Moscow is **big**. So big that there are three airports you can arrive to.

As soon as you get to the exit of any one of them, you will get swarmed with taxi drivers offering you a ride. Unless you are three or more, go through them and straight to the Aeroexpress train.

Aeroexpress train will take you to one of the Moscow subway stations for mere 420 rubles (the price is valid for 2017, but shouldn't increase too much later either). The trains are fast and comfortable, and you don't face the risk of anyone scamming you.

If you travel in a larger group, you may consider taking a taxi together. Make sure you agree on the price beforehand. And make sure the driver means this price for the whole group, not for each person in the car. Getting unbelievable amounts of money from naïve foreigners is among the last pleasures left for these poor guys after the Aeroexpress system started operating.

6. PUBLIC TRANSPORT

The subway system in Moscow is called Metro (Метро) and is your go-to place as a guest in the city. The train system is pretty straightforward and easy to use. You pay for entering Metro and can make as many switches between the lines as you want until you exit. Trains come every minute or two and have free wi-fi in them.

Metro is open from 5.30 am to 1 am every day. All the passenger announcements and station names are dubbed in English, so it's probably the most tourist-friendly place in Moscow.

When you ask a Muscovite where they live, they usually reply with the closest subway station. So learn the one you stay close to, it will help you a lot.

The cheapest way to buy tickets is paying 50 rubles for the Troika card. You can charge it with as much money as you need in one of the service machines or at a cash desk in the Metro. Then you just have to push it against the sensor to enter Metro, buses, trams, or trolleybuses – they are all parts of the same payment system.

7. EVERYONE IS A TAXI

Proper taxis are only for very rich people. Because you can get exactly the same service for a way smaller price if you aren't lazy.

It is common in Moscow to just stretch your arm out and wait for the cars to stop by you. Regular drivers can bring you wherever you need for the price you negotiate, especially if it's on their way. There is always a tiiiiny little chance you will end up in the trunk of the car, but what is life without adventures?

Uber works perfectly fine here too. Around 5 competing services popped up soon after it appeared, so the rates were pushed down pretty low. You can get from one side of the city to another for around 400 rubles even in the middle of the night.

8. APPS TO DOWNLOAD

Yandex is the Russian version of Google, and it has all kinds of useful apps too. And in Russia, they work a bit better.

Yandex Navigator will tell you how to get anywhere by car and how long it will take you. Moscow's traffic is terrible, and Yandex always has the current information on the traffic jams all around the city.

Yandex Metro will show you the subway map and let you plan your route and switches.

Yandex Transport will help you with the rest of public transport. It even tracks buses in real time.

Google Translate will help you with these intimidating Cyrillic letters. I didn't know it myself until recently, but you can take a photo of the text you need to translate and it will do it for you. Perfect for shop signs.

And get one of the taxi apps. Uber, Yandex Taxi, MyTaxi or any other one works totally fine.

9. SHOPPING NEVER SLEEPS

For whatever you need, you can find a place in Moscow where you can buy it 24/7. I have personally found myself sitting in a queue at the dentist's at 1 am once.

Every district has smaller grocery stores and pharmacies that operate at night. You might need to google the place first if you want something like a power drill, though.

Shops and restaurants work during weekends and holidays too. Bars don't close till the morning either. I guess Moscow tourism office should target insomniacs with their advertising.

10. RED SQUARE, KREMLIN, PUTIN, LENIN

No, I'm not playing "find the odd one out" with you. All of these are concentrated in the very center of Moscow and are one big tourist classic worth spending your afternoon around.

The Red Square – Krasnaya Ploshyad' (Красная Площадь) - used to host bustling markets, but now it's bustling with tourists trying to get a nice picture. To be fair, that's quite easy. St. Basil's Cathedral – Sobor Vasiliya Blazhennogo (Собор Василия Блаженного) - is that famous colorful temple you see on all typical books about Russia. Right next to it are the red walls of Kremlin. You can go inside through one of the towers or walk around and check the Eternal Fire at the Tomb of the Unknown Soldier. You will find it by the crowd of people waiting for the next changing of the guard.

Kremlin houses current government buildings including Putin's secret office, as well as historic temples and relics. You can find Tsar Cannon - the largest bombard in the world, and Tsar Bell – an enormous bronze bell that has never been rung. Check out the museums on the territory if you want to see some really cool weapons and jewelry of the old.

Lenin's Mausoleum also stands proudly on the Red Square. Rumors say that no one born in Moscow has ever been there, but every immigrant has. That is due to the complicated opening times, so check in advance. And yes, Vladimir Lenin's dead body is really on display there.

11. SHOPPING AND SIGHTSEEING COMBINED

After a walk around Kremlin, take a break at GUM (ГУМ) - a historical shopping center on the Red Square. It used to be the main place to go to for Moscow shoppers, and it's still one of the fanciest ones. It has beautiful interiors and nice tourist-friendly shop assistants (which is not that easy to find in Russia).

Visit the lemonade stand to choose one of the colorful syrups for your own Soviet beverage. The flavors will definitely be a new experience for you.

For a full meal, go to the top floor and find Canteen 57 (Столовая 57). It's a replica of a typical Soviet canteen with all the dishes my parents and grandparents used to eat with great pleasure so often.

If your pockets are about to burst from all the money, go to TSUM (ЦУМ) nearby. This shopping gallery has clothing and accessories from top brands and designers worldwide, and is an important landmark in itself.

12. I FOLLOW THE MOSKVA, DOWN TO GORKY PARK

If you know the Scorpions, you must have heard this park's name. Gorky Park used to be a traditional area for walking and chilling during Soviet times; then it became the main amusement park in Moscow. Now, all the rides were taken away, and it became the meeting point for the youth who have any interests besides drinking and videogames. Hipsters, too.

Gorky Park has an area for skating and parkour, a football field for amateur teams, an area for petanque, a gallery of modern art, and a nice pond you can rent a pedal boat at. And it's all surrounded by trees and food trucks. Beautiful and tasty.

The park is located on the bank of the Moskva river, and there is a fascinating glass bridge going over it. If you've got balls of steel, you can even climb on top of its steel beams outside to truly enjoy the view. Sometimes the security guards may try to stop you, though.

In the winter, Gorky park gets covered in ice for one of the largest ice skating rinks in Moscow. Muscovites love skating down its icy roads, with occasional pit stops for mulled wine and a burger.

Andrey Artyushin

13. MOSCOW AT NIGHT

Moscow is known as the city that never sleeps. That's why it starts shining with millions of lights once the night falls.

During winter times, Moscow undoubtedly becomes a sight that's better to see at night. Join one of the many boat tours along the Moskva river to see the city center from the water.

Or just take a cab from one side of the city to another and squeeze your face against the window. Make sure Kremlin and the Cathedral of Christ the Savior – Khram Khrista Spasitelya (Храм Христа Спасителя) - are included in your driver's route.

14. HOW TO FEEL LIKE A SNOB

Moscow has all those cultural entertainment spots where people don't really enjoy going but go nonetheless to appear sophisticated and intellectual. But if you genuinely love opera and ballet, or perhaps fine art - man, have I got a treat for you!

Bolshoy Theater is a beautiful classic building in the center of Moscow. It is the place for the most renowned opera and ballet performances in the world. Or for dressing up fancy and gazing at marvelous interiors. The prices really bite, so if you are in purely for the performance, you might want to check some less historical theater.

Tretyakov gallery is where you go for classic art. Its collection is enormous, and you can learn everything you want about Russian fine art. Muscovites genuinely love this place. Last winter, people queued up for hours to see the new temporary exhibition they brought in. And I remind you, it was **Russian** winter. Emergency services had to be called in to make sure the art lovers don't freeze to death.

Andrey Artyushin

15. SOVIET FACTORIES AND MODERN ART

In Moscow, when you want to see modern art, you go to a factory. Two large factory areas have been bought by art spaces and now host the exhibitions of the cutting-edge international and local artists.

The names are Vinzavod (Винзавод) – literally, "wine factory" – and Artplay. They are located in the same district and you can check both of them out in one go to see what's new in the art world. The large factory spaces worked out perfectly for displaying grandiose paintings, sculptures, and other enormous art objects. Artplay also hosts lectures, rooftop concerts, and various design stores where you can buy anything from a cool poster to a golden bathtub.

Or go to one of the branches of MMOMA – Moscow Museum of Modern Art. Each building has a different collection, and you can find some of the more classic modern art too, like Picasso and Dali.

16. ROOFTOP TOURS

Moscow is said to be built on seven hills, but we don't really have many mountains you can look down on the city from. But we have many tall buildings, and you can climb on top of some of them.

Of course, the cool local guys know some roofs that are easy to access or are not heavily guarded. But you don't have time for checking all the local rumors, so just take a rooftop tour.

Some experienced roofer will take you on several rooftops around the city and show you the breathtaking views. Maybe tell some interesting stories, too. You can even arrange a romantic date on a rooftop, which is a pretty sweet way to see the sunset.

Andrey Artyushin

17. BEAUTIFUL UNDERGROUND

Moscow Metro is one of the oldest and most alluring subway systems in the world. Its deep stations used to serve as bunkers during World War II, and still carry many reminders of the communist era.

Many of the stations have bright ceiling frescoes, impressive statues, or thematic hall decorations on them. Check which ones to look out for online, or book a tour and let a professional guide tell you about the history that Moscow citizens walk above every day.

18. WORLD'S LARGEST FRIEND ZONE

VDNKh (ВДНХ) is an enormous Soviet-time exhibition area themed after international friendship. Each pavilion was built by a different Soviet republic to showcase their crafts and economy.

Apart from these exquisite old buildings, there is an amazing golden fountain (also in the name of friendship) and **an actual spaceship**. And if that's not enough for you, check one of the crazy exhibitions they have around the park. There is always something like live sharks or robots to see. And a real bunker from the cold war times.

On the way from the Metro station (also named VDNKh), take a look at the sky-high building of the Museum of Cosmonautics. It's easy to notice - it looks like a rocket flying up into space.

Not too far off is the famous Worker and Kolkhoz Woman monument. It used to be a logo for a Soviet film studio, a part of the Olympics opening ceremony, and a prototype for the Magic is Might statue in Harry Potter. And it's just a breathtaking huge statue you should definitely see once in your life.

Andrey Artyushin

19. 360° VIEW FROM THE TV TOWER

You can see the 540-meter tall Ostankino TV tower from most parts of the city. So you really can't say you couldn't find it.

There are tours to show you around the tower and tell you all about Russian television. But what you really shouldn't miss is the restaurant – Sed'moye Nebo (Седьмое Небо).

They built its 3 floors at more than 300 meters above the ground, and they **made them spin**. So you can enjoy your meal while slowly rotating around the tower and watching Moscow from above. That might be the highest merry-go-round in your life.

20. MODERN JOURNEY THROUGH JEWISH HISTORY

Probably the most modern and interactive museum in Russia is located on Maryina Roscha (Марьина Роща) station. It's called the Jewish Museum & Tolerance Center and it's pretty fun.

You can walk through all the stages of Jewish history and interact with the digital exhibits at every step. Start with the 4D theater that will give you the perspective on the origins of the Jewish nation. Then walk through a model of a typical Jewish shtetl and take a seat at an Odessa café table to hear some interesting stories from the Imperial Russia times.

I won't spoil the rest of the exhibits for you, so you'll have to trust me on this one: even if you have never felt an urge to learn about Jewish culture, this museum will make you spend a couple of hours walking and learning history the fun way.

21. COUNTRY OF HARD LIQUORS

Don't know if you've heard about it, but Russian people love vodka. Yes, don't be shocked, it's really true.

Of course, we are the motherland of vodka. That's why it's cheaper and tastier here. Try brands like Belenkaya (Беленькая), Green Mark (Зелёная Марка) or Bulbash (Бульбаш) for something affordable and nice.

We also love brewing hard liquors on herbs and berries to get different types of schnapps and moonshine.

Nastoyka (настойка) is a general name for flavored hard liquor you can usually find in restaurants. You can try such flavors as lemon, honey, horseradish, cranberry, and many others.

Samogon (самогон) means it's a homemade alcohol, like moonshine. It can be very delicious and range from 30 to 80 percent alcohol.

Basically, go to the hard liquor page, choose anything that sounds unfamiliar, and embrace the Russian adventure.

22. RULES ABOUT ALCOHOL

Despite the whole reputation, Russia is not a total alcoholic's paradise where you can drink whenever and wherever you want.

Alcohol is sold only from 8 am to 11 pm in the stores. Unless the store has a bar license, then it can sell it 24/7. One like that is Gastronom (Гастроном) on Akademicheskaya (Академическая) station.

The legal drinking age is 18, and the constant checkups on alcohol sellers made them ask you for your ID even if you are stumbling on your own beard.

It's not legal to drink on the streets or in public places like parks. Technically, it should be ok if you put your bottle in a paper bag, but not all the policemen know it. So better hide your booze when you see the police to be on the safe side.

23. PUB CRAWL WITH SIGHTS

Here is my tested and approved path for your pub crawl.

1. Get out of Kitay-Gorod (Китай-город) station in the direction of Solyanka (Солянка) and go into the side street behind a red church. The name is Slavyanskaya Ploschad' (Славянская Площадь) and it has 4 or 5 good bars to start your night with. If it's a weekday, Stay True bar has a 2-for-1 offer on cocktails after 5 pm.

2. Go up the boulevard behind a large statue of two men until you turn right to the Maroseika (Маросейка) street. Walk along it, stopping at any tapas or wine bar you see. Zolotaya Vobla (Золотая Вобла) is a cheap beer bar where you can stop for a quick authentic Russian snack and watch some football.

3. Walk until you get to the crossing with Chistoprudny Boulevard (Чистопрудный Бульвар) and turn left. You'll find two bars to the right: Ukuleleshnaya (Укулелешная) and Cuba Libre (Куба Либре). Ukuleleshnaya is a ukulele showroom and a bar combined, with original drinks and dishes. And Cuba Libre is just a nice spot to get your Latino mood going with some rum and dancing.

4. Enjoy the view of the ponds, and walk on down the boulevards until you reach Sretenka (Сретенка) street. Don't stop yourself from checking any bars on the way, but try to end up in Crazy Daisy – the wild and chaotic place where everyone dances on the bar, and offers like unlimited alcohol for 200 rubles happen monthly.

24. CLUB ISLAND

Strelka (Стрелка) is a spot on the Moskva river where the crème de la crème come to party. The top luxurious clubs like Icon, Gypsy, and Rolling Stone are all close by together here for you to pick and choose.

Russian face control is probably the fiercest in the world. You have to put on your best clothes to get into these bars. And you only have one shot – they remember you and won't let you in even if you change and come later the same night. Being a foreigner may help, though.

And for God's sake, don't catch a cab on Strelka or close to it. There are drivers waiting all night long to charge the club goers 5 times the normal rate.

25. ROCK OUT CHEAP

Punk is still not dead in Moscow. Concerts for as little as 300 rubles are still easy to find in clubs around the city.

Just google "punk concerts Moscow" or whatever genre you are interested in to check out all the bars that can let you enjoy the beer, the music, and the mosh pits.

The concerts in Moscow always start at least an hour after the official starting time. But you can join the crowd for predrinking with store-bought booze in front of the concert venue.

The pubs to check are Glavklub (Главклуб), Glastonberry pub, Plan B, 16 Tons, Theater (ТеатрЪ) and Chinese Pilot Jao Da (Китайский Лётчик Джао Да).

26. CRAFT BEER STREET

Let those taps flow! Maliy Gnezdnikovskiy (Малый Гнездниковский) side street is your go-to place for draft & craft.

Craft republic is known to be the best craft beer bar in Moscow, but there are several other interesting places with hipster names around it, like All Your Friends (Все Твои Друзья), Howard Loves Craft, and Too Much Beer and Wine.

Head to Chelsea GastroPub for some quality food when you want a break from all the beer. But you know the thing about craft beer bars — they always have a bunch of snacks you've never heard of.

Andrey Artyushin

27. SECRET BUNKER BAR

To find this bar, you have to go into a narrow side street, find the entrance into what used to be a bomb shelter, and then press a button that reads, "call the cat". Then, the smoke will start coming and the walls will open to reveal the entrance to the Schrödinger's Cat bar (Кот Шрёдингера).

This speakeasy has more surprises waiting for you on the inside too. The cocktail card is designed as the periodic table of elements, categorizing the original alcoholic mixes by the main ingredient and percentage of alcohol. Each experimental drink is served in its own special container – you can get anything from a trophy cup to a plastic bag.

And of course, they didn't forget about the whole Schrödinger theme. Food comes in boxes, and you don't know what's inside till you open. But, to my experience, it's not a dead cat. Usually.

28. PARTY BEHIND BOLSHOY THEATRE

Some bars in Moscow are very Russian, and some are very European and international. This one is both.

Kamchatka (Камчатка) bar and club is situated right in the center of Moscow, just two minutes from the Bolshoy Theatre. You can always find a pretty international crowd in there, despite the atmosphere inside being so chaotically and destructively Soviet Russian.

Enjoy the shots with names like Brain Tumor and Getting Wasted With Pikachu, or go hard and take thematic sets of 10 shots or more straight away.

Russian salads and open sandwiches compete with grilled meat and sausages for your attention on the menu. Try hunter's set of cured meat, including deer, pork neck, beef, chicken, and horse.

The music is a wild mix of the 90's and 2000's hits, so it's very unlikely you'll stay seated at your table for long.

29. THE NEW BREED OF RESTAURANTS

Moscow has recently become the home for the new type of restaurants and bars. True Cost has 3 locations in the city, but they have already patented their concept and are waiting for the world to catch on. Because it seems to be working.

The concept is simple – you only pay for the actual price of the ingredients of the dish, not the typical restaurant marked-up price. That means you get top cuisine and cocktails for just a handful of rubles. You can buy something as mouth-watering as BBQ chicken wings with carrot and blue cheese sauce for mere 140 rubles (2 euros) and get cocktails for a third of the usual price.

The trick is, you have to pay a fixed price at the entrance. During the day it's just 150 rubles, which is almost nothing, but it grows to 500 rubles during the weekend and evenings.

So get your appetite together and make sure you order enough to make the entrance price worth it.

30. GET A MUSHROOM IN YOUR LEMONADE

I can't offer you much info about magic mushrooms, but I can easily tell you about the place where there are so many mushrooms it's magic.

The restaurant is called Mushrooms, and it has all kinds of dishes cooked with truffles and forest mushrooms. Even soft drinks and desserts.

To add to the experience, Mushrooms is located on the rooftop of a mall almost in the center of Moscow. The view, the comfy interior, and the unusual dishes are definitely worth the above-average prices.

31. TRYING RUSSIAN CUISINE

A typical Russian meal is something you can't easily stand up after. So that's why it's important to try it in a place where it feels nice to sit inside.

Mari Vanna (Мари Vanna) is stylized to look like a typical Moscow flat from the past. It has its own "flat owner" and even pets to make you feel welcome and cozy.

Ilya Muromets (Илья Муромец) has the atmosphere of an even older period of Russian history. You'll see hay decorations, waiters in traditional peasant clothes, and maybe a mini pig. Yes, the mini pig is not a very historic animal, but it's absolutely adorable, so who cares.

The dishes to try are:

Pelmeni (пельмени) - Russian meat ravioli
Julienne (жульен) - a metal pot with mushrooms in creamy cheesy sauce
Solyanka (солянка) - a salty and sour soup made out of everything left in the fridge
Syrniki (сырники) - sweet little quark pancakes served with sour cream and jam
Borsch (борщ) - the classic Russian red soup they screw up abroad
Olivye (оливье) - the classic "Russian salad" invented by a French chef

Kholodets (холодец) – jelly with meat inside. You want a story to tell your friends, don't you?

32. AMAZING GEORGIAN FOOD

Georgians are known in Russia for being amazing chefs. And they never fail to prove it. Moscow is full of wonderful Georgian restaurant, and you really can try any of them and have the best time of your life.

My personal favorite is Khachapuri (хачапури) café network. They have all the dishes you need to try, and they cook them deliciously.

The signature snack of the place is the khachapuri (not surprisingly). It's Georgian cheese bread that can be prepared in about 7 different ways. Don't worry about which one to choose, any of them will make you go crazy. And take some Georgian wine with it for even more orgasms in your mouth.

Apart from that, you can pick any dish on the menu and it won't be a miss. Minty sauces, smoky flavors, exquisite ingredients like pomegranates and grape leaves…I'm going for some Georgian right now.

Andrey Artyushin

33. GIVE DÖNER ANOTHER CHANCE

Even if you are tired of all the döner kebabs and dürüms you find everywhere at home, Moscow shawarma (шаурма) is from another world.

I have tried the stuff at many döner places around Europe, but nothing compares to the way they make it here. The wrap is soft and crunchy, meat is flavorful, and the shawarma chef will put a bit of spicy and white sauces on top to make your first bite nicer – isn't that a sweet touch?

You can always choose if you want to wrap it in regular laffa bread or the cheese one. But we still need more scientific research to check if there is more to the difference than just the orange color.

34. FAST FOOD TO DISCOVER

Don't just go to McDonald's or KFC, try one of the brands you'll never find again!

Kroshka Kartoshka (Крошка Картошка) serves baked potatoes with delicious fillers. The right amount of different fillers per potato is four. And the sandwhiches here are on point.

Teremok (Теремок) is the place to try bliny (блины) – the Russian pancakes. The prices are quite democratic, even if you take one with caviar. Traditional Russian porridges for breakfast are pretty nice here too.

Russian donuts – ponchiki (пончики). Not a brand, just the type of pastry you have to try from a street vendor. Tastes like churros, but less sticky.

On second thought, try McDonald's too. They have the cheese sauce for the fries here, which is **heavenly**.

Andrey Artyushin

35. SURPRISES IN GROCERY STORES

Every time I visit home, I have a shopping list of tasty things to bring abroad from here. Fine, I'll share it.

Sguschyonka (сгущёнка) – sweetened condensed milk. Goes well with anything, tastes better than anywhere.

Malosol'niye Ogurtsi (малосольные огурцы) – semi-pickled cucumbers. The golden middle.

Calamari (кальмары) – dried calamari you eat as a beer snack. Salty and juicy.

Ikra(икра) – caviar. Cheaper here than anywhere. Most people prefer the black one to red, but it costs more too.

Kvas (квас) – bread cola. Tastes like something between dark beer and Pepsi. Might be an acquired taste.

Grechka (гречка) – buckwheat. A very popular side dish to eat here, tasty and nutritious.

White bread, mayonnaise, sour cream. Yes, you have it abroad, but they are different here. Mayonnaise is tastier, sour cream is creamier, and white bread…it just looks cuter.

36. TOP RESTAURANT IN EUROPE - LITERALLY

In Moscow city, there is an area called the Moscow City. It sounds confusing, but in reality that's a bunch of huge glass skyscrapers crowded together you can't miss.

Most of these are filled with offices, but there is some space for fun and fancy dining too.

Sixty is a pop-art style restaurant with a view that's hard to find. Sixty is located on the 62nd floor. Logic is not the most treasured thing in Russia.

It's said to be the highest restaurant in Europe, so perhaps the pricey dishes are worth it.

37. EXPERIENCE SOCCER

Soccer is the most popular sport in Russia, even though we suck at it. Moscow has many stadiums that are pretty easy and cheap to get into.

Try getting a ticket for one of the fan zones, especially for a match with heated rivalry between the teams. The soccer might not be very impressive, but you will definitely be moved by the energy of the fans. Screaming, singing, and illegal fireworks are always there to enjoy. And maybe even some fighting. The kind of fighting you should really watch from afar.

The police control is pretty tough. If you manage to get fan tickets for a team from a different part of Russia, you might even get a walk through a live corridor of cops on horses and with police dogs all the way from the Metro.

38. WHERE TO WARM UP IN COLD RUSSIA

When drinking vodka and putting another layer of fur on is not enough, Russians go to the sauna.

Traditional Russian sauna – banya – is a fiery-hot wooden room with coals where people beat each other up with short brooms and call it pleasure. No, I'm not joking.

But there is a more luxurious option too. Sanduny (Сандуны) is the oldest sauna complex in Moscow. It still keeps its authentic interior decoration style from 1896 and remains as fancy as a sauna can get.

And yes, they can beat you up with a broom here too.

Andrey Artyushin

39. ARCADE FROM BEHIND THE IRON CURTAIN

No, we didn't have Pac-Man in USSR. But we had our own arcade machines, and they still function.

Museum of Soviet Arcade Machines is the place for real old school gamers. You get a bunch of Soviet coins at the entrance and are welcome to play the classics from the 80's and 90's.

There are driving simulators, sports games, and even shooters. Just please have pity on the poor oldies and don't button mash.

40. STARRY SKY IN THE METROPOLIS

It's pretty hard to see any stars with all the lights in Moscow. But there is one spot where you can see them even during the day.

Yes, it's a planetarium. But this one is pretty cool. The cinema inside used to be my number one place for romantic dates. You lie down in soft chairs and gaze at the night sky projections all over the huge dome above you.

The permanent exhibition is quite interesting too. It's a pretty modern collection of scientific experiments you can interact with. And meteorites. Don't tell me you don't think space rocks are cool.

Andrey Artyushin

41. IT'S THE CITY OF ESCAPE ROOMS

The escape room boom took Moscow by storm several years ago, and now you can find all kinds of these quests around the city.

There are ones for kids and ones that scare the hell out of you, ones with live actors who beat you up and ones where you have to destroy stuff yourself.

There are many brands that provide this experience in English, so google away! I've seen a room set in 1941 and one with the Harry Potter theme available already, so there is definitely something to choose from.

42. THERE'S NEVER ENOUGH CHURCHES

Or so it seems to Moscow government. There are almost 600 temples and churches in Moscow, and I really doubt there is someone who has visited them all.

You can easily spot them by their golden domes shining in the sun. And the largest one is within walking distance from Kremlin.

The Cathedral of Christ the Savior – Khram Khrista Spasitelya (Храм Христа Спасителя) - is pretty remarkable in its size and stature. Especially considering it was demolished in the 30's.

It is more of a tourist place than a holy place these days, so don't be shy and take a look at the exquisite golden interiors and altars. It's easy to get lost in all the catacombs and balconies inside. And the bridge going from the temple and across the river must be the best place to take a beautiful photo in Moscow.

Andrey Artyushin

43. ICE SKATE UNDER THE WALLS OF KREMLIN

If you find yourself in the middle of winter Moscow, take advantage of your chilly situation and find an ice rink. There are many of them in every district, with children skating and playing hockey until they can't feel their face.

There are also bigger ice rinks with rentals, and they are so beautiful that people come there in thousands.

VDNKh, Gorky Park and Sokolniki Park (ВДНХ, Парк Горького, Парк Сокольники) get huge territories covered with ice and get very pretty shiny decorations to surround them.

The Red Square hosts one every year too. It's smaller, but definitely fancier. You can even find shows like traditional dancing or ice drifting if you come during the day. And it's just a marvelous and heartwarming experience whatever time you come.

44. HOW TO SKI IN JULY

We have several small ski resorts around Moscow you can drive too. But only one that works all year round.

Snej.com (Снеж.ком) is a ski slope that is **inside.** It feels really weird to walk on snow when it's +35°C outside, but you can do it here.

It has a proper chairlift and rental service too. And an ice skating rink. In case you really miss winter.

45. GET USED TO RUSSIAN SERVICE

In Soviet Russia, vendors don't have to be nice to you – you have to be nice to vendors.

I want you to remember: it's nothing personal. They just don't see the point of being nice to you – it's you who needs to buy something from them, after all. So be efficient, ask for what you need and you'll get it. Sometimes not. Then raise your voice and get scary. That's not even considered rude.

Restaurant service got way better in the recent years, but you still should ask for your bill in advance. The customary tipping amount is 10%, but no one will get upset if you don't tip at all.

46. GET TO KNOW SOME RUSSIANS – AND GET DRUNK WITH THEM

The best way to have some fun time in Moscow is to get to know some crazy Russians. That's not as hard as it may seem.

Foreigners are still a rarity in Moscow. And cool strangers with a desire to have some real adventure are harder to find than bad vodka here. We are all welcoming hosts by nature and we truly enjoy showing people around.

So don't be afraid to approach someone at a bar and ask some questions about Russia or Moscow. Just submit to what happens next. You are very likely to get some free drinks, end up at some house party with people who don't even speak English, and wake up somewhere you have no idea how to get home from.

47. FESTIVALS IN MOSCOW

We love holidays in Moscow. Unlike in Europe, everything operates on public holidays too – you can use shops, supermarkets, everything. Here are the main events throughout the year:

New Year – 31st December.
In Russia, New Year is the biggest holiday and the time to give presents – not Christmas. Every flat gets a fir tree, the streets get covered in special decorations, people roam the streets - it's sweet. On the New Year night, the whole city center gets crowded. Because at midnight, the main clock on one of the Kremlin's towers strikes 12 and a huge fireworks display starts.

Victory Day – 9th May
It's a celebration of the victory in World War II. It starts with a massive parade on the main square, with tanks and planes and the whole shebang. People visit war monuments and city parks in general to remember the veterans and honor the dead. The government spends millions on cloud seeding – a technique that makes sure the rain falls outside of Moscow and doesn't reach it on the day of the festival. So it's always a nice day to spend outside.

Maslenitsa – early March
This holiday comes from the pagan times when people celebrated the coming of spring. The main thing we took from it is the pancakes – you are supposed to eat a lot of them, and man, they are delicious! You

can find them at numerous street markets at this time of year, where people come to eat and see some old Russian traditions recreated.

48. HOW NOT TO WASTE YOUR MONEY

Moscow can be the cheapest or the most expensive place to visit. For anything you want, you can find the places that charge crazy money and the places that basically let you steal it.

Resist your urge to go to the places that have English signs and menus outside – they are usually overpriced tourist traps. In general, it's a good rule for going around the city center to only go to places located on the side streets.

Avoid yellow taxis and choose bars where you see and hear drunk people from afar – they are your best bet for cheap drinks.

49. LEARN SOME PHRASES

Where is …?   Gde…? (Где…?)   Gde Metro? Where is the Metro?

Excuse me/ I'm sorry Eezveeneetye   (Извините) Eezveeneetye, gde Metro? Excuse me, where is the Metro?

I don't speak Russian Ya nye govoryu poh roosky (Я не говорю по-русски)   Eezveeneetye, ya nye govoryu poh roosky.

I'm sorry, I don't speak Russian. Thank you Spaseebo (Спасибо)

Please/You are welcome   Pozhahloosta (Пожалуйста)

How much is this?   Skol'ko ehto stoeet?   (Сколько это стоит?)Eezveeneetye, skol'ko ehto stoeet?bExcuse me, how much is this?

50. SAFETY TIPS

Your trip to Moscow should work out fine if you use the common sense. Don't leave your things without supervision, don't go into shady empty streets at night, don't get too close to drunk guys - stuff like that. The actual muggings are pretty rare these days, but scamming isn't. Don't be a naïve tourist. If a stranger in a touristy area starts actively talking to you and tries to make you go somewhere or do something, better say no and leave.

Carry your real ID at all times, not the copy. The police get picky about that. They don't get too picky about other stuff with foreigners because they usually don't speak good English. You can often be let go for minor violations once the policeman finds out you don't understand Russian.

Being gay is not illegal in Russia. But if you are homosexual, you should really avoid public displays of affection, especially if you are male. You may easily get beaten up for that, Russian people are pretty bigoted this way, unfortunately.

There is a lot of ignorance going on when it comes to racism, so you might hear some remarks that you'd find offensive. But there is no hate behind them, people just don't know better.

Be careful near the roads, too – the traffic is crazy. Cars are not very happy to let the pedestrians pass, so look out when you cross.

Oh, and don't drink the tap water!

Andrey Artyushin

TOP REASONS TO BOOK THIS TRIP

History: Hear the stories of Tsars, Dictators, and Presidents.

Food: All the dishes and ingredients you haven't tried or even heard of.

Culture: Experience the 1001 ways mentality and customs are different here.

Stories to tell: Come back with stories about your crazy Russian adventures.

>TOURIST

Andrey Artyushin

> TOURIST
GREATER THAN A TOURIST

Visit GreaterThanATourist.com:
http://GreaterThanATourist.com

Sign up for the Greater Than a Tourist Newsletter:
http://eepurl.com/cxspyf

Follow us on Facebook:
https://www.facebook.com/GreaterThanATourist

Follow us on Pinterest:
http://pinterest.com/GreaterThanATourist

Follow us on Instagram:
http://Instagram.com/GreaterThanATourist

Andrey Artyushin

> TOURIST
GREATER THAN A TOURIST

Please leave your honest review of this book on Amazon and Goodreads. Thank you.

We appreciate your positive and negative feedback as we try to provide tourist guidance in their next trip from a local.

NOTES

Printed in Great Britain
by Amazon

83351826R00048